Kamal El-Mallakh

CAIRO
GIZA - SAKKARAH - MEMPHIS

97 Colour illustrations

BONECHI

Kamal El-Mallakh,
architect, Archeologist,
Egyptologist,
discovered mainly the
solar boats of the great
pyramid. He is on the
board of 20
international
comities for Egyptology
and professor on
several universities.

* * *

© Copyright
CASA EDITRICE BONECHI
Via Cairoli, 18/b
FLORENCE - ITALY

Printed in Italy by
Centro Stampa Editoriale Bonechi.

ISBN 88-7009-231-3

Photographic service by:
LUIGI DI GIOVINE

Photos of pages 26, 27, 28
(below), 29, 33 by:
GIANNI DAGLI ORTI

Translated by:
M.A. Bakeer

CONTENTS

CAIRO

Egypt was the first state to establish a system of administration and a capital where the administrative and religious centre lies.

During the late Predynastic Period, Confederations started to emerge with political heads or kings and a capital. In Lower or Northern Egypt, the capital was Buto in the heart of the Delta. The king wore a red crown with a cobra as an emblem. In Upper or Southern Egypt, the capital was Nekheb between Aswan and Luxor; the king of which wore a white crown with a vulture as an emblem. The papyrus plant and its flower were the symbol of the North, while the lotus plant and its flower were the symbol of the South.

Then came the unity between the North and the South under the reign of King Menes (or Narmer) who chose Memphis between the north and the south to be the first capital of unified Egypt. Memphis is 22 km from Cairo.

The best place for the foundation of the Egyptian capital was always the point before the Nile branches. The capital of Egypt has changed throughout history from Ahnasia south of Memphis to Thebes (Luxor).

When Alexander the Great entered Egypt in 332 B.C., the capital was transferred west of the Delta to Alexandria. Christianity was introduced and the seat of the Patriarch was between Alexandria and old Cairo.

Alexandria remained the Egyptian capital during both the Ptolemaic and Roman periods.

In 639 A.D. Amr Ibn El As entered Egypt and introduced Islam. He wanted to keep Alexandria as the capital of Egypt but Khalif Omar Ibn Al Khatab ordered him to build a new city. He founded Al Fustat in 641 A.D. beside the fortress of Babylon as the first Islamic capital of Egypt.

When the Abbassides took over from the Ommayades in 750, Saleh Ibn Aly abandoned Al Fustat and established Al Askar north of the former capital. This new military capital developed and constituted with Al Fustat a big city.

Ahmed Ibn Touloun founded the third Islamic capital Al Qatai around his gigantic mosque in 870. This city had also a military character, with its high walls and circular road. Quickly it formed with Al Askar and Al Fustat, one city.

When Gohar Al Sikkily, the Fatimid commander entered Egypt, he built the new city of Al Qahira or Cairo in 969 and from then on it became the capital of Egypt and the heart of Islam.

Since the foundation of Al Fustat and until the construction of Cairo, capitals (cities) were always constructed to the north. Therefore Al Qahira was constructed north of the three cities built by the Arabs.

This is the beginning of a long period during which the city grows in dimensions. In effect a new capital develops quickly and passes its limits.

The arrival of Salah El Din in 1176 marks a different stage in the history of Cairo. During the Ayyoubide era, the Citadel was built and work began on building a wall surrounding the cities forming Al Qahira.

The Mameloukes era (1250-1517) was a period of great construction and town planning in Cairo. The Ottomans (1517-1798) continued the development.

The Mameloukes began adding big commercial activities. During the reign of Mohamed Aly and his successors, the city developed considerably.

After the revolution of 1952, and in the sixties, there was a great demographic growth in Cairo.

Greater Cairo today houses twelve million inhabitants, and is composed of three governorates: Cairo, Giza and Qalyobia, as well as twenty eight quarters.

The average density of population is 50,000 inhabitant/km².

The historical capital is considered the most populated African city. It is also a great political, cultural and economic centre in the Middle East.

THE CITADEL
OF SALAH-EL-DIN

During 9 centuries this fortress dominated the eastern side of Cairo over the Moqattam hill. It was the place of residence of Mohamed Aly Pasha who governed Egypt from 1805 to 1848.

He constructed his beautiful Mosque with its two high minarets after 23 years of his reign that lasted for 43 years. No one looks at the citadel without remembering two incidents, the first when the king of Cyprus was taken captive and had to pay his ransom to Mamlouk Bersbay to gain his liberty. The other incident is the massacre of the citadel arranged by Mohamed Aly Pasha on the 1st of May 1811 after 6 years of reign in order to get rid of his rivals, the Mameloukes. Mohamed Aly had them all invited on the occasion of the declaration of his son Tosson, Chief of the Egyptian Military expedition against the Wahhabis in Saudi Arabia. The great banquet took place in Al Gawhara palace. After feasting they were leaving on horseback but when they descended, Mohamed Aly's guards shot and killed them. The gates were all closed and there was no escape. All were killed except one who galloped back up the ramp and leapt off the ramparts with his horse.

THE MOSQUE OF IBN KALAOUN

East of the Mosque of Mohamed Aly stands the Mosque of Sultan Al Nasser Ibn Kalaoun who was one of the sultans of El Mamalik El Baheria. The mosque was constructed in 1318 and reconstructed in 1335.

The western portal holds an engraved inscription bearing the date of its first construction. There is another engravement over the northern portal bearing the date of its second construction.

The mosque is composed of a courtyard surrounded by four iwans. The biggest is that which faces the «kibla» or towards Mecca. This iwan is composed of 4 corridors boarded with 4 rows of columns.

The other two iwans have two corridors each boarded with two rows of columns.

In the middle of the «kibla» iwan there is a great mihrab covered with fine marble and decorated with nacre. The cupola of the mihrab rests over granite columns and wooden stalactites. It is covered with green mosaic and from here came its name «The green cupola».

The interior walls of the mosque were covered with marble and encrusted with nacre at a height of 5 meters. There is very little left of these ornamentations. The ceiling is covered with coloured pieces of wood. The mosque has two minarets in different styles. Their domes are adorned with mosaics and they are of exceptional beauty.

Sultan Kaitbay restored the mosque in 1471 and the cupola in 1488.

Joseph's well (Bir Youssef)

Behind the mosque there is a spiral well 90 meters deep with two stages. The first is 50 meters deep and the second 40 meters deep. This well was used during wars. Water was raised by means of Sakiah (a water wheel that works by oxen to raise water).

Soft water was provided by means of a canal that ran through the wall of the citadel which stretches to Fustat. Traces of this canal can still be seen today.

The Mosque of Souliman Pasha

This mosque is also known by the name of Sariat El Gabal. It is situated on the north west side of the Citadel. Built by prince El Mortadah Magd El Khelafa, it is the first mosque in Egypt to be constructed according to the Ottoman style. In 1528 it was restored by the Mamelouke Souliman Pasha El Khadem.

It is composed of two sections: the eastern part designated for praying. It is surmounted by a cupola surrounded by semi-domes richly ornamented with painted designs and verses from the Koran written in different calligraphic styles.

The cupola is covered from the outside in green mosaic.

The western part has an open courtyard. There is an inscription bearing the name of the constructor and the date of construction.

The court is surrounded by 4 iwans with coloured cupolas 16 meters high.

The Egyptian Antiquities Organisation set up a restoration scheme of the Citadel in 1982. It also founded a museum for the royal vehicles that belonged to Mohamed Aly's family. These vehicles were used by Egypt's kings until 1871, when the Khedive Ismail left the citadel. On one of the museum's walls there is a big painting of these vehicles in a procession on the occasion of the opening of the Suez Canal.

There is also the archaeological museum in the garden that covers 9000 meters. It has a display of columns in the Islamic style. There is also a shop selling antiquity reproductions. The Egyptian Antiquities Organisation also founded a centre for the restoration of Islamic and Coptic monuments and there are excavations in two different places in the court of the Citadel. One is at the north of the court near the cupola of the Sidi Mohamed El Kaaki south west of the mosque of Souliman Pasha. The other is near the entrance gate on Salah Salem Street east of the Citadel.

The Citadel has been flood lit from the outside and a garden is cultivated on the eastern side.

MOHAMED ALY MOSQUE

Mohamed Aly Mosque is the emblem of the Cairo Governorate. Mohamed Aly (1769-1849) was born in Cavalia, Greece, and was of Albanian origin. He was a soldier in the troops that were sent to Egypt to free the country from Napoleon's occupation and took part in the land battle of Abou Kir on the 25th of July 1799. In 1808 he was the commander of the Albanian troops in Egypt.

In 1805, Egyptians revolted against Wali Khourshid and Mohamed Aly took over.

The mosque was built in 1830 in two parts: the mosque and the courtyard.

The court measures 52×54 m and is surrounded by four corridors lined with marble columns and surmounted by little domes. In the centre of the court there is the fountain for ablutions (where muslims wash before saying their prayers that take place five times a day). The clock tower on the

western side of the fountain is of perforated copper. The clock was a present from King Louis-Philippe of France to Mohamed Aly Pasha in the year 1845.

Architect Youssef Boshna from Turkey who executed the construction of this mosque, took his model from the Hagia Sophia, the church that was later transformed into a mosque, and is known for its Byzantine style.

The mosque is square in shape, the length of its side is 41 m, the central dome is 21 m in diameter and 52 m high. It is supported by 4 square pillars and surrounded by 4 semi-domes and the semi-dome of the kibla.

On the western side of the mosque stand two cylindrical minarets (pencil minarets) in the Ottoman style. The height of each is 84 m.

This mosque is characterized by the great quantities of alabaster that adorn the walls. The pulpit (minbar) and the dekka (tribune) are made of white marble. The mihrab is covered with alabaster and gold decorations.

A large number of pendant glass and crystal lamps form circles of lighting inside the mosque.

Tomb of Mohamed Aly Pasha

The three tiered tomb of Mohamed Aly Pasha is at the right side of the entrance door of his mosque. It is made of white marble, decorated with carved floral motifs and covered with painted and gilded inscriptions.

Mosque of Sultan Hassan on the left and Al Rifaii Mosque on the right.

MOSQUE OF SULTAN HASSAN

This is one of the most beautiful and monumental mosques in Cairo. The builder of this mosque and school is Sultan El Nasser Hassan. He is the 19th of the Turkish Sultans to have reigned in Egypt and the seventh son of the Sultan El Nasser Mohamed Ibn Kalaoun.

Conspiracies were one of his era's traits. He decided to build his mosque in the square facing the

Citadel of Salah El Din. He began the construction in 1356 and it was completed in the year 1363 by Bashir Agha who was one of his princes. This mosque is considered one of the greatest works of Islamic architecture. The mosque is 7907 square meters wide. The entrance is 37.80 m high.

There is also a school or a madrassa mosque for the four rites of Islam.

The court is almost a square in shape. Each side is about 32 meters in length. On each side there is an iwan that stands higher than the court. Each iwan is roofed with a brick-pointed tunnel-vault with a stone arch. Art lovers consider the arches of its largest iwan a miracle of construction.

The walls of the Iwan are covered with coloured stone blocks and marble. There is a stucco inscription containing verses from Surat El Fath in Kufic writing. In the middle of the iwan there is a marble pulpit and tribune of great craftsmanship. Around the mihrab there are four marble supports.

On the right side of the minbar, which is made of white marble, there is a wooden door covered with bronze. At each side of the qibla wall there is a door. The two doors lead to the tomb chamber. The doors were covered with bronze and gold silver inlay.

The tomb chamber is 21 square meters large and 50 meters high. The walls are covered with marble up to 8 meters.

The Mosque of Sultan Hassan has two minarets. One is 82 meters high and is considered one of the highest Islamic minarets. It is two meters shorter than the two minarets of Mohamed Aly Pasha Mosque which was built 500 years later.

Tasteful architectural decoration abounds in the interior of the Mosque of Sultan Hassan east of Cairo.

AL RIFAII MOSQUE

It is the most famous mosque in Cairo built by a lady, Princess Khoshiar Hanem, Khedive Ismail's mother. Khedive Ismail, who attended the inauguration of the Suez Canal, made many great renovations in Cairo. The mosque was completed in 1912.

Al Rifaii Mosque is in the north of the mosque of Sultan Hassan. Between the two mosques is the Citadel Road (sh. El Qalaa) leading to the big square of Salah El Din.

Al Rifaii Mosque resembles in many architectural elements the mosque of Sultan Hassan. The site, chosen by Princess Khoshiar, was occupied by the Al Rifaii family which goes back to Imam Ahmed Al Rifaii. This family and its subordinates were famous for their spiritualism and their ability to master snakes and vipers. From there the name of this mosque was derived.

Al Rifaii mosque occupies an area of 1767 square meters. It is flanked by four massive piers with pointed arches dividing the mosque into 3 porches. The mosque contains a big cupola. In the middle of the eastern wall there is a big mihrab. There are two marble columns on either side, one is white and the other dark green. The mihrab is decorated with mosaic work of fine marble and nacre. Most of these materials were imported from Europe. The minbar and the Koran stand are made of Indian wood chopped and collected together with ivory, ebony and nacre inlays.

The mosque houses the vault of the late royal family of Egypt beginning with Khedive Ismail Pasha and his mother, Princess Khoshiar, up to King Farouk the First.

Tomb of the Shah Mohamed Reza Pahlavi

The Late President Sadat invited the late Shah to stay in Cairo during his illness after the rejection he met from other countries during the Khomeini revolution against his throne. He died and was buried in June 1980.

The Shah's father was also buried in the same place when he died during the second world war in Ethiopia. His remains were transferred back to be buried in Iran.

Tomb of Farouk the first

The last king to rule Egypt abdicated his throne in July 26, 1952 and died in April 18, 1965 in Italy. His body was brought back to Egypt during Nasser's era to be buried in an unknown tomb. President Sadat then ordered the burial of his remains in the family tomb of Al Rifaii mosque.

IBN TOULOUN MOSQUE

This is one of the biggest mosques in Cairo.

It was constructed between 876 and 879 by Prince Ahmed Ibn Touloun, the founder of the Toulounid dynasty. He founded the 3rd Islamic capital of Egypt Al Qataii over Yuchkour hills, around his gigantic mosque, south east of Cairo. The mosque is an imitation of the huge mosque at Samarra in Mesopotamia.

The city of Al Qataii was divided into allotments where different troops lived, old allotments of the Sudanese, the Romans, etc.

The mosque is a square in shape and measures 162.5×161.5 m. At the centre there is a big courtyard which is almost a perfect square measuring 92.5×91.80 meters. The courtyard is surrounded on all sides by galleries (riwaks) and the kibla is in the biggestone. There is an outer courtyard surrounding the mosque on three sides called ziyadat.

The mosque is built with baked bricks to protect it from fire and water. The arches of the galleries rest on brick piers covered with a thick layer of plaster with engaged brick columns at each corner.

There are 129 windows in the mosque made of plaster with filigree decoration representing geometrical and floral designs.

The minaret which is exceptional in design is 40 meters high and the outside staircase is spiral following the same model of the minaret of the Samarra mosque in Iraq.

It is said that the architect of the mosque was a Christian from Syria who also built the intake tower of the aqueduct that served Al Qataii. When he heard that Ahmed Ibn Touloun wanted to build his mosque without robbing the churches of their columns, he expressed his desire to fulfill Ibn Touloun's dream.

At the eastern corner of the mosque stands the Gayer-Anderson museum or Beit-El-Kreatlia that dates back to the Mameloukes' period (about 1630). These two adjoining houses belonged to the El-Kreatlia family from Crete. The last owner sold them to the government who in turn gave guardianship of the building to the Englishman Gayer-Anderson. He began restoring and refurnishing them with precious furniture in the Arab style. Their interior decoration mainly follows Mamelouke themes. Other collections have been added since then. There is a Chinese room, a room in Queen Ann style and a hanging garden.

The Necropolises east of Cairo.

THE NECROPOLISES

Contrary to the Pharaonic tombs that were dug and erected on the western side of the Nile valley, these tombs are situated on the eastern side of the valley at the foot of the Mokkattam Hills. Tombs of the Fatimids, 1000 years old, can still be found. Tombs of the Caliphs are found near Bab El Nasr (door of Victory). Some of these go back to the Circassian Mamelukes' period in the 14th and 15th centuries.

The Mosque of Sultan Barkouk is situated north of the Necropolises. It covers an area of 73×73 m, and dates back to the beginning of the 15th century. The Mosque of Qait Bey was built by the Sultan in 1474 south of the Necropolises. Its minaret is 40 m high. Many members of the royal family are buried south of the citadel near the tomb and mosque of Imam El Shafeie, which was built in 1211 and is famous for its beautiful cupola.

Funerary mosque of Qait Bey.

Mosque of Sultan Barkouk.

AL-AZHAR MOSQUE

This is the most famous mosque, not only in Egypt, but in the Islamic World. It is also the biggest international Islamic Centre where students coming from all over the world receive their academic and theological studies. It is considered the oldest Islamic university and the most important centre for teaching the Arabic language.

Gawhar El Sikilli began the construction of the mosque in 970 A.D. (359 of Hegira) during the reign of the Fatimid Khalif El Mouiz Lidin-Illah. The first Friday prayers and Khoutbah took place in 972 A.D. (361 of Hegira).

In the beginning, the mosque consisted of three Iwans surrounding the court. The biggest is the Kibla Iwan which is composed of 5 galleries.

There are several riwaks that served as lodging rooms for students divided by province or country. The most important riwaks were those of the Abbassides, Teibarsiah, Kurds, Indians, Bagdadians, Turks, Maghrabians, Syrians, Saidians (students from Upper Egypt), the Hanifites, the Hanbala, the Gawharia ... etc.

There are 8 gates in Al-Azhar Mosque, the most important of which is that of Bab El Mouzainin (gate of the barbers).

One of the minarets had been constructed by Sultan Qait-Bey in 1458. The second, on its left, is by Qansuh El Ghouri. It is divided into 16 faces contrary to other minarets that have 8 faces only. It is covered with mosaic and is double pointed.

Al Mosqui street, one of the most ancient markets of Cairo with its small shops selling textiles and other goods. The street leads to the famous tourist bazaar of Khan Al Khalili, near Al Hussein Mosque.

STATUE OF RAMESSES II

It was found in Memphis, then was taken to Cairo in 1954, to be exhibited in the station square. It is 10 meters high and the double crown represents the unity between the North and the South. On the back of the statue there is a stanchion bearing the Pharaoh's titles, one of which is «The Strong Ox» which is the symbol of fertility. Between the statue's legs is a relief of Ramesses' wife (Bent-Anath) who was, at the same time, one of his 200 sons and daughters and one of his three daughters who were given this title. A replica of this statue stands now on the road leading to Cairo Airport.

THE EGYPTIAN MUSEUM

The French Egyptologist, Mariette Pasha, insisted on the construction of a big museum housing the Pharaonic works of art. Twenty years later, the French architect Marcel Dourgnon presented the plan of the Egyptian Museum building situated in the centre of Cairo. The museum was opened in 1902 and Gaston Maspero was appointed manager. The museum contains a big library and 100 exhibiting rooms occupying two floors. In the museum's garden, there is a big bronze statue over the marble tomb of Auguste Mariette bearing his name and dates of birth and death (1821-1881). There is also a number of statue representing other famous Egyptologists. The most important collection of the museum is that of Tutankhamun. There are other masterpieces belonging to the Ancient Kingdom like the Statues of Cheops, Chephren and Mycerinus. There is also the collection of Thoutmous the Third, Akhnatoun and a number of statues of Ramesses the Second.

The main entrance of the Egyptian Museum

Two statues on either side of the gate represent the symbols of the North and the South of Ancient Egypt. One is holding the lotus and the other the papyrus.

The gold coffin of Tutankhamun

The gold coffin of Tutankhamun is made of 450 pounds of solid gold. It is, perhaps, the finest and greatest work of goldsmith in history. Three coffins were used to store the body of young king Tutankhamun who died at the age of 18. The inner and outer coffins are displayed among his collection in the Egyptian Museum in Cairo. King Tut's tomb was discovered in November 4, 1922 by British Howard Carter, after six years of hard work underneath the rubble that heaped up during the excavation of King Ramesses VI tomb, in Thebes, Valley of the Kings.

Gold mask of King Tutankhamun (Dynasty XVIII)

It weighs 9 kgs of solid gold and was placed over the head and shoulders of the king's mummy.

The stripes of the headdress are made of blue glass which was used also for the inlay of the fake beard. The vulture's head upon the brow, the symbol of sovereignty over Upper Egypt is also made of solid gold and the beak is of lapis lazuli. By its side there is the cobra, the symbol of sovereignty over Lower Egypt. Its body is made of solid gold and the head of lapis lazuli. The hood is inlaid with carnelian, lapis lazuli, turquoise, coloured glass and quartz. The eyebrows, eyelids and kohl marks are all made of lapis lazuli and the eyes of quartz and obsidian.

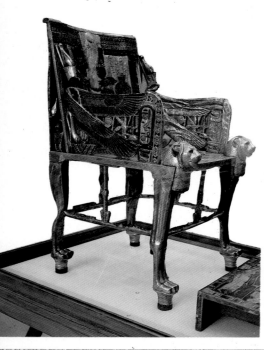

One of King Tut's throne chairs (18th dynasty)

The effect of Tal Al Amarna art is reflected on this piece of art. This kind of art was well known during the reign of King Akhnatoun, King Tut's elder brother, who was, at the same time, his father in law.

On the back panel of the royal throne there is a scene representing King Tut and his wife the queen, standing before the seated king and touching him gently on the shoulder while the solar disk is shining above them. It is made of wood plated with gold and silver and coloured glass paste inlays; a thing that was very rare.

Queen Nefertiti (18th Dynasty)

An unfinished work of brown quartzite, 51.5 cm high with traces of coloring. This is the head of the famous queen Nefertiti, wife of King Akhnatoun, who called for the worship of one God.

Sheikh El Balad (Dynasty V)

This is the most famous wooden statue belonging to the Old Kingdom. It is the statue of noble Kaaper who was also known as the great priest. You can see the dignity reflected on his features. The eyes are made of quartz embedded in copper lids. It is made of a single block of sycamore wood, apart from the arms. When it was found in 1860 near Sakkarah, it reminded the workers who discovered it of their «Chief of the Village» or «Sheikh El Balad», the mayor's assistant, hence its name.

The Scribe (Dynasty IV)

Ancient Egyptians considered the profession of the scribe to be the highest of professions. The scribe was close to the Pharaoh because of his wisdom and knowledge. This statue is made of painted limestone and is of an unknown squatting scribe holding an open papyrus roll on his knees. The eyes are of inlaid quartz and framed with bronze. Although the ancient Egyptian was very careful to keep up with artistic standards in sculpture, there is a little deviation of the statue's head to the right side as if thinking before writing.

Dwarf Seneb and his family (Dynasty VI)

The ancient Egyptian sculptor excelled in this piece of work of the Dwarf Seneb, who was an important official, and his family. He portrayed Dwarf Seneb with his wife holding him with her right arm and their two children in the place of the dwarf's short legs. This group is made of painted limestone and was found in Seneb's tomb in Giza north of Chephren's pyramid.

King Mentuhotep (Dynasty XI)

This is a rare statue of Pharaoh Mentuhotep of the 11th dynasty. It is one of a group of eight statues that were found in his mortuary temple at Deir Al Bahary, west of Luxor, beside Queen Hatshepsut's temple built five centuries later.

The sandstone statue, which is 2.3 meters high, represents the Pharaoh seated in the Osiris position wearing a white costume with his crown painted red. The colour of the body under the white cloak is olive black. The statue was found wrapped in bandages like a mummy and placed in a funerary niche in his monumental temple.

Prince Rahotep and his wife Nofret (Dynasty IV)

This statuary group that was found in the tomb of Rahotep in Meidum represents Prince Rahotep, who was high priest of Heliopolis, and his wife Princess Nofret. They are carved out of two separate blocks of limestone, but were meant to be seen together. They are both painted, with inlaid eyes and in an excellent state of preservation. One can notice that usual distinction in colour between the skin of men and women that was usually made by ancient Egyptians.

A group of black granite (Dynasty XVIII)

This is a group of black granite representing the major Senefer of Thebes sitting beside his wife Senetnay with their daughter Mutneferet between them. It dates back to the 18th dynasty during the reign of Amenhotep the 2nd.

33

MODERN CAIRO

As the saying goes: Egypt is the Gift of the Nile, and indeed this is true. Since the dawn of history, great civilizations developed along its banks. The Nile penetrates the heart of Cairo, Egypt's capital, and is considered one of its great features. There are four islands in the Cairo Nile, two of which are inhabited.

Big buildings and international hotels flank the two banks, giving modern Cairo a new image. Among the important buildings overlooking the Nile is that of the Egyptian TV and Broadcasting Organisation and that of the Arab League. Five main bridges have been constructed to connect different parts of the capital and to overcome the problem of heavy traffic which is a major concern in most capitals of the world. There are five universities in Cairo. The oldest and most famous is that of Al-Azhar. The other four were constructed at the beginning of the 20th century.

There is also an academy of art that houses institutions for studying cinematic and theatrical arts, ballet, and a conservatoire.

The history of the cinema in Egypt began in 1926, and there are fifteen studios that produce more than 360 films annually. There are 15 theatres, 3 circuses and more than 40 cinemas.

World famous musician Verdi composed his «Aida» opera to be presented at the opening of the Cairo opera, which was burnt in the seventies. A new opera house is being constructed in Guezirah, a donation from Japan.

There is a number of museums in Cairo, most important of which are the Egyptian Museum, the Coptic Museum, the Islamic Museum and the Agricultural Museum.

The Cairo Zoological garden is considered one of the biggest and oldest zoological gardens in the world. There is also the Andalucian garden, the Orman garden, the Horeya gardens, and the Japanese garden of Helwan.

Cairo Guezirah tower is considered the symbol of modern Cairo. Architect Naoum Shebib designed it and construction began in 1957. It is a cylinder 187 m high, faced with a concrete network which opens at the top taking the form of the lotus flower, the symbol of ancient Upper Egypt and one of the themes of ancient Egyptian art. On the 14th floor there is a revolving restaurant, on the 15th floor there is a cafeteria, and on the 16th floor a viewing platform and a panorama over Cairo and its suburbs.

Left: one felouke over the Nile; right: Cairo Guezirah Tower.

CAIRO AND THE NILE

Greater Cairo is considered the biggest city in the Middle East and Africa in area and in population. 11 million inhabitants live in Greater Cairo at night and 12 million during the day.

The Nile runs in the middle of the city. Coming from the south, it passes through Nubia, Aswan, Luxor, Abydous, Tal Al Amarna, Beni Hassan, Menya and Memphis on the outskirts of Cairo. Then it is divided into two branches forming the Delta before it pours in the Mediterranean.

There are four islands in the Cairo Nile, two of which are inhabited. The biggest island houses a lot of international hotels and important buildings as well as gardens, sporting clubs, museums and last but not least the Cairo Tower.

Next pages:
View of the garden in which the National Museum of Egyptian Civilisation in Guezirah will be built.

The Nile bus is passing in front of Nile Hilton Hotel.

6th October Bridge.

General view of the east side of Greater Cairo.

AL MOALLAKA CHURCH

The church is known by the name of Al Moallaka or the suspended as it rests upon columns. It is also known by the name of the Church of the Blessed Virgin. The church is built on the ruins of the fortress of Babylon which the Romans erected to serve as a defence centre between Upper and Lower Egypt.

You can visit the church now through the garden of the Coptic Museum in Misr El Kadima (old Cairo) or through its main entrance facing the Mari Girgis station.

The church is constructed according to the Basilican order and is surmounted by two towers. In the 11th century, it served as the seat of the Coptic patriarch.

There is a flight of stone stairs leading up to the church from the ruins of the fortress. All its pillars are in white marble except for one which is in black basalt. The pillars form three rows and they date back to the fourth century A.D.

The most impressive wood relief in the church is that representing Christ entering Jerusalem and the festivities taking place on Palm Sunday. It is now exhibited in the Coptic Museum.

The pulpit of the church is made of marble and there are three altars (Haykals); the centre one was dedicated to the Virgin Mary, the southern one to the St. George and the northern one to the St. John the Baptist.

The church was restored several times, the latest of which took place in 1984.

The gate of the Moallaka church is decorated with stucco floral motifs. In the centre there is the inscription: «Glory to God» in the Arabic language.

ST. SERGIUS CHURCH

It is one of the most famous Coptic churchs and is considered the most ancient of Old Cairo. The church was constructed on the site where the Holy Family took refuge, during their flight into Egypt when they visited the place.

Here in this church the election of Shenouda, the 55th Patriarch, took place in 859, as well as the election of Abraham the 62nd Patriarch in the year 977.

The church, built according to the basilica style, has 12 marble columns, one of which is in granite.

The church is as restored in the year 1982 by the architect Joseph Zaki of the Egyptian Antiquities Organisation.

CHURCH OF ST. BARBARA

Constructed in 684, it houses the relics (remains) of Saint Barbara.

It is remarkable for its fine iconostasis with its metal motifs and coloured designs.

The church furniture was transported to the Coptic Museum to be exhibited.

COPTIC MUSEUM

The Coptic museum was founded in Old Cairo beside the Babylon fortress in 1910. This site in Old Cairo was chosen because of its association with the beginning of Christianity in Egypt.

The museum is surrounded by six ancient churches of particular importance: Al Moallaka - St. Sergius (Abou Serga) - St. Barbara - Mari Girgis - The Holy Virgin and the Church of Kasriat Al Rihan, which was burnt in 1975.

The Coptic museum contains a collection of the most ancient Coptic objects from churches, palaces and coptic houses, as well as architectural fragments and ancient gospels. This collection belonged to Marcos Pasha Smeika.

The museum is composed of two pavilions and a courtyard which is a museum in itself exhibiting Coptic architectural elements. The old pavilion was erected in 1910 and the new one in 1947.

The old pavilion features balconies (mashrabia) and wooden ceilings brought from ancient coptic palaces, as well as fountains, stucco and mosaique windows, marble and limestone pillars.

The museum is composed of 29 rooms exhibiting frescoes, wood carvings, metal work, pottery and glass work, tapestry, papyrus, manuscripts, stationery, icons and ivory productions.

There is also a library that holds 7000 books, volumes and manuscripts, the majority of which are in the Coptic language. The others are in the Amharic or Arabic languages.

At the entrance of the museum, there is a fountain

covered with a wooden cupola, according to the arabesque style of the «Mashrabiah» that is supported by 4 marble pillars. There is a chandelier suspended from the vault (arch) with 366 small lamps representing the number of days in the year.

In the niche behind the fountain, there is a fresco representing Christ on his throne, surrounded by 4 angels. Between the saints Michael and Gabriel, there are two faces. One is illuminated, symbolizing the day; the other is obscure, symbolizing the night. Under the faces there is a representation of the Virgin holding her child.

The base of the fountain is in black and white marble triangles.

Aphrodite

At the right side of the entrance, in room I, there is a work of rare beauty, representing Aphrodite, the Goddess of beauty in Greek Mythology (Hathour in Pharaonic Egypt). Her neck is encircled by a necklace with a pendant, and a floral wreath crowns her head.

Room III.

Most of the pillars are in limestone, with their floral capitals influenced by Byzantine art. These columns are displayed in room III and were brought from Coptic palaces and churches or ancient Coptic convents in Egypt.

Room VI

The pillars of the Coptic era are characterized by the simplicity of their bases and the interlaced decoration of their capitals representing vine leaves.

This is a picture of the pillars in room VI brought from the Monastery of St. Jeremiah in Sakkarah.

There is a pulpit with two small columns surmounted by a stucco window coloured in red, yellow and cobalt blue.

Fresco of Adam and Eve

You will find this wall painting in room IX. It is considered one of the most famous masterpieces in the Coptic museum. The fresco represents Adam and Eve in paradise eating the forbidden fruit, followed by their fall when God ordered them to descend to earth.

Over the fresco of Adam and Eve there is a stucco window surmounted by a cross. Light enters through the coloured glass with its birds and floral designs. The wooden ceiling in the room is brought from one of the ancient Coptic houses and is characterized by its interlaced woodwork.

This room also contains a niche with coloured stucco designs representing the Virgin carrying her child with two angels, one on each side. The niche is surmounted by a frieze of aconite branches.

The wooden staircase leading to the second floor is decorated with cross and fish motifs, symbols of Christianity.

Room X

It contains different collections of masterpieces like ancient gospels in both Coptic and Arabic languages with coloured pictures.

There are also manuscripts of Saints, decorated with floral motifs and some inscriptions in Arabic and Coptic languages. One of these inscriptions says: «In the name of God, the Merciful, the Compassionate».

You will also find ancient booklets of papyrus, two manuscripts in papyrus of St. Thomas's gospel mentioned in the library of «the Knowers of God» which is composed of 13 books that were found in the «Hamra Dom» village near Nagah Hamadi in Upper Egypt dating back to the third and fourth centuries A.D.

The room also exhibits five manuscripts in the Coptic language dating back to the 6th century A.D. as well as a roller in the Amharic language.

The room contains inkpots, bamboo pencils and the four gospels in both the Arabic and Coptic languages.

Half the rooms are designed for coptic textiles. One of the remarkable tapestries is that of the «Flute Player», woven with cotton and woollen threads according to the Coptic style. This tapestry dates back to the fourth century A.D. and was found in the Village of «Sheikh Ebada» near Miniah in Upper Egypt.

MUSEUM OF ISLAMIC ART

It is one of the most important museums in Cairo. Situated in Bab El Khalk square, this museum was inaugurated in 1903. It houses masterpieces of Islamic art.

Room 16 is one of the most remarkable. It exhibits faience and ceramic vessels of different styles. One can find more than 68 styles of incrusted and perforated designs over faience productions. There are designs representing Coptic symbols like the fish, as well as Islamic geometric designs. You will also find faience productions of the Mameloukes' era, bearing slogans of their different troops and dating to the 14th century. This room exhibits a chimney of the Ottoman style that dates back to the 18th century.

The carpets hanging on the walls are of different Turkish styles, as well as reproduced stones that were used in the decoration of the Ibn Touloun Mosque in the 12th century.

There is also a display of Persian and Turkish turquoise tiles that go back to the 17th and 18th centuries, as well as pottery productions of Samarkand with the Chinese influence of the 12th century, and porcelain productions that were found in Mameloukes' mosques.

A door with silver decorations and a big bolt. The floral bas-reliefs in Turkish style decorate and frame the 4 angles of the door. The name of the artisan «Jahovah Asslan» is engraved in the middle. The back of the door is simple in design. It contains 8 decorated parts and an iron bolt.

There are 15 exemplars of the Koran in the Museum of Islamic Art. Here is a manuscript on deerskin in «Kufic» writing that goes back to the Ommayad era. It is part of the collection of the Prince Omar Sultan that dates back to the 7th century.

The Museum is famous for its wood and metal works. The walls of one of its rooms are covered with woodworks fitted together without the use of nails or glue. A pendant lamp spreads light over a copy of the Holy Koran.

This pot in bronze was found beside the tomb of Marwan Bin Mohamed in Persia in the first century of Hegira (7th century A.D.). It is 41 cm high and its spout is made in the form of a cock crowing. It is considered one of the masterpieces in the museum.

A copper chandelier composed of three parts, one over the other. The tray underneath was used to receive the oil of its lanterns to prevent it from dropping over the heads of people performing their prayers.
It was named after Sultan Al-Ghouri and was made by the artisan Mohamed Al Mawardi in the 15th Century AD (9th Century of Hegirah).

Replica of Imam Al Husseim tomb that goes back to the Ayoubite era in the 13th Century AD (7th Century of Hegira). It is made of a special kind of Indian wood. Its fine woodwork is fitted together without the use of nails or glue reflecting the genius of Islamic artisans and the magnificence of Islamic art.
The Islamic inscriptions are a contribution of Kufic and Ayoubite calligraphies.

51

GIZA PYRAMIDS

To the west of Greater Cairo stands the plateau of Giza that holds Egypt's historical mark... The three pyramids and the Sphinx.

The three pyramids are tombs of three pharaohs representing three generations of the pharaonic fourth dynasty beginning with Cheops, the second sovereign of the fourth dynasty and ending with Mycerinus.

The three pyramids are situated on the left bank of the Nile. Their funerary temples were constructed on the east side of each pyramid and their entrances were always at the north facing the North Star where the paradise of good spirits exists.

Inside each pyramid and on the east side there is a chamber or serdab for the statue of the deceased king. On the west side there is a chamber designated for the sarcophagus.

Orientation was very important to the Ancient Egyptians. The east signified rebirth while the west signified the empire of the dead.

In general, all pyramids belonging to the old kingdom are oriented on the four cardinal points with great precision.

The great pyramid of Cheops

It was considered by the ancients one of the seven wonders of the world. King Cheops had it erected to serve as a tomb for his royal body. 100,000 men worked for twenty years during his reign that lasted for 24 years to accomplish this piece of art. Almost 2 1/2 million blocks of limestone were used for building.

The pyramid of Cheops was originally 146 m high, but it decreased in height and now it is 137 m high. The side of its square base is 250 m long. The incline is 51°.52.

The original entrance is blocked and the hole made by tomb thieves is being used. There was a funerary temple on the east side of the pyramid and a causeway connected it to the lower temple where purification ceremonies and mummification took place.

The original entrance to the pyramid of Cheops.

The pyramid of Cheops.

There are five solar boat pits associated with the Great pyramid, three of which are cut out of stone, while the other two, discovered by Kamal El Mallakh in 1954, are made of wood. Pharaohs had three boats erected to enable the soul to sail to heaven in an everlasting trip within the sun procession.

The pyramid of Chephren and the Sphinx

The pyramid of Chephren is the second of the Giza group. It is situated on the south west side of the great pyramid of Cheops.

This pyramid gives the impression of being higher than that of Cheops because the plateau on which it stands is slightly higher at this point. It is built on a square of 210×210 m. Its apex today reaches 136.5 m but was originally 143 m. The incline is 53˚.10.

King Chephren tried to cast his pyramid with granite blocks but he died before achieving his goal. One third of the cast can still be seen at its summit.

The complex of this pyramid is similar to that of the great pyramid. It has two entrances facing the north.

There was a small queen pyramid on the southern side of the pyramid but its stones were robbed in the middle ages and there is no trace of it now.

The valley temple of King Chephren is near the Sphinx or Aboul Hul as the Arabs call it. The body is that of a lion with a human head that is considered an effigy of King Chephren. The beard and nose are missing.

It is 20 m high and 73 m long. The width of the face is 4 m.

The pyramid of Cheops.

The pyramid of Chephren.

The pyramid of Mycerinus
and the three queen pyramids.

The pyramid of Mycerinus

The third pyramid of the Giza group is that of
Mycerinus. The pyramid was originally 66 m high
but today it is 62 m high. The side of its square base
is 108.5 m long and the incline is 51°. Granite
blocks cover 16 courses of the pyramid.

A sarcophagus in bazalt was found in the funerary chamber and inside there was a mummy in a
wooden case. They are displayed in the British Museum in London.

The usual complex is found near the pyramid,
valley temple, causeway and funerary temple. There
are three queen pyramids on its southern side; the
height of each is not more than 10 m.

Beautiful groups of Mycerinus were discovered
near the funerary temple in the thirties. Most of it is
on display in the Egyptian Museum of Cairo.

SAKKARAH

Sakkarah is 20 km south of Cairo. It is named after Soker the God of the Dead. Sakkarah is situated west of Memphis and its necropolis is the greatest of all Egypt.

Step Pyramid of Sakkarah

King Zoser, the founder of the third dynasty and the old kingdom, constructed his step pyramid in 2730 B.C. It is the first pyramid in history. The architect was Imhotep, High Priest and famous as a doctor, such a man of genious that the Greeks, two thousand years later, deified him under the name of Esculapius.

The pyramid is 60 m high and the king's tomb is at the bottom of a large vertical shaft 28 m deep. The tomb was adorned with blue faience. The pyramid is composed of six steps and from there was derived its name. The base is a rectangle measuring 121 m×109 m.

The pyramid complex is surrounded by a wall 10 m high. It is decorated with recesses and false doors. At the entrance there is a large colonnade which is composed of 40 columns which is the number of provinces of Ancient Egypt, each joined to the side wall by means of a small connecting wall. The height of each is 5 1/2 m.

There is a vast court to the south where you can find altars. There are three interior courts, one with halls for the celebration of the Heb-Sed jubilee festivities, as well as House of the South and House of the North. Then there is the southern tomb. Under this complex there is a number of underground chambers (serdabs) where 30 thousand beautiful vessels of alabaster were found.

The necropolis of North Sakkarah houses several Pharaonic pyramids, the most famous is that of King Unas (2310-2290 B.C.). The walls of the central chamber and the tombs are covered in hieroglyphic texts arranged in columns and painted in blue. The inscriptions are known as the Pyramid Texts. There are a collection of magico-religious texts to allow the dead Pharaoh to face his rebirth after death.

The Serapeum

Auguste Mariette discovered the Serapeum or the sepulchre of the mummified sacred Apis bulls in 1851. This rock-hewn sepulchre is on the north east side of the step pyramid. It dates back to the Amenophis III era. On both sides of the main underground gallery there are niches, each containing a granite sarcophagus of the Apis bull that weighs about 60 tons.

In the Ptolemaic period an open space was adorned with statues of Greek philosophers and great men of wisdom.

Beside the Serapeum there is the Mastaba of Ti that belonged to a high court official from the Vth dynasty. There are also the ruins of the Monastery of St. Jeremiah (5th century Coptic Saint). It was built by coptic Egyptians in the fifth century A.D. The ruins include 2 churches as well as 2 press houses for olives and grapes.

Mastaba of Mereruka

Around the step pyramid standing on the Sakkarah plateau there are several pyramids that were constructed during the old kingdom and a number of tombs belonging to members of the royal family and big officials. Among these is the Mastaba of Mereruka, discovered in 1893.

An important official, who was also a priest, constructed the tomb of Mereruka at the beginning of the sixth dynasty for himself, his wife Hert-Watet-Khet and their son Meri-Teti. It is the largest tomb in the area (40 m×24 m). It contains 29 rooms and

is divided into three parts for himself, his wife and son.

The tomb is decorated with murals representing scenes of daily life in Egypt including the different Egyptian professions and scenes of hunting birds, fish, hippopotamus and crocodiles from the river Nile, as well as animals creeping between papyrus branches. To the right of the entrance you can see Mereruka portrayed painting the three deities representing the three seasons of the Egyptian year: the flood, cultivation and harvest. You can see him once again represented on his skiff and lying on his bed next to his wife who is playing the harp.

On an opposite wall there are dancers performing a variety of movements.

You can see below a mural representing a scene of how animals were fed.

MEMPHIS

Menes, the founder of the first dynasty 5200 years ago, chose Memphis as the Capital of Egypt after uniting Upper and Lower Egypt under his rule. Thus Memphis became the first capital in history.

Memphis with its few existing ruins is situated 25 km south of Cairo and is now the two villages of Mit Rahina and Badrashein. After the end of the Old Kingdom it remained the residence of great Pharaohs: Snefru, Cheops, Chephren and Mycerinus. It was also the political centre of the country. Its tombs were scattered to the North in Sakkarah.

One of the most important features of Memphis now is the Sphinx that represents Amenophis II. It is 8 m long and 4.25 m high and weighs about 80 tons of limestone. It stood at the entrance of the Temple of Ptah.

Colossal statue of Ramesses II (Dynasty XIX)

Earthquakes have thrown it on the grounds of Memphis. It is made out of one block of limestone that crystallized with time. The statue is displayed in a special museum there. Its height is about 14 m if completed because one arm and part of the legs are missing. Now it is 10.30 meters high. Its ear is 50 cm long. There are royal cartouches engraved on its shoulders, hand and girdle where you can find a dagger decorated with two falcon heads. On the sides, there are representations of some of his sons and daughters.

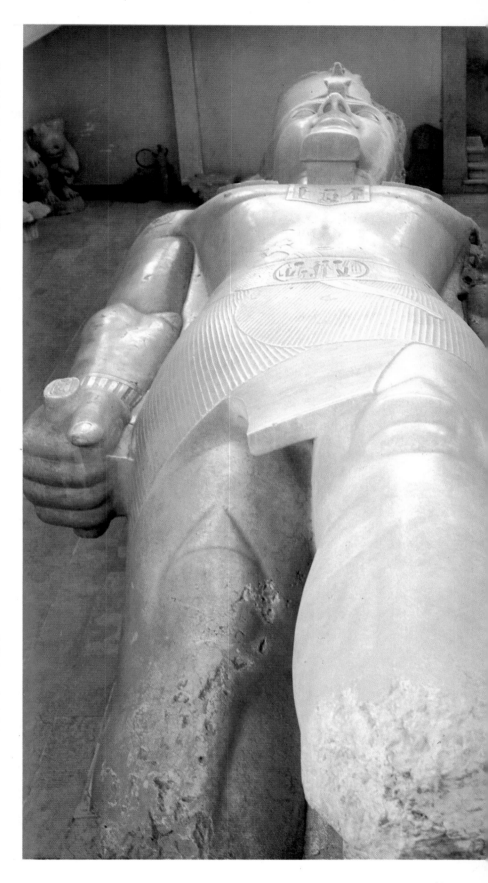

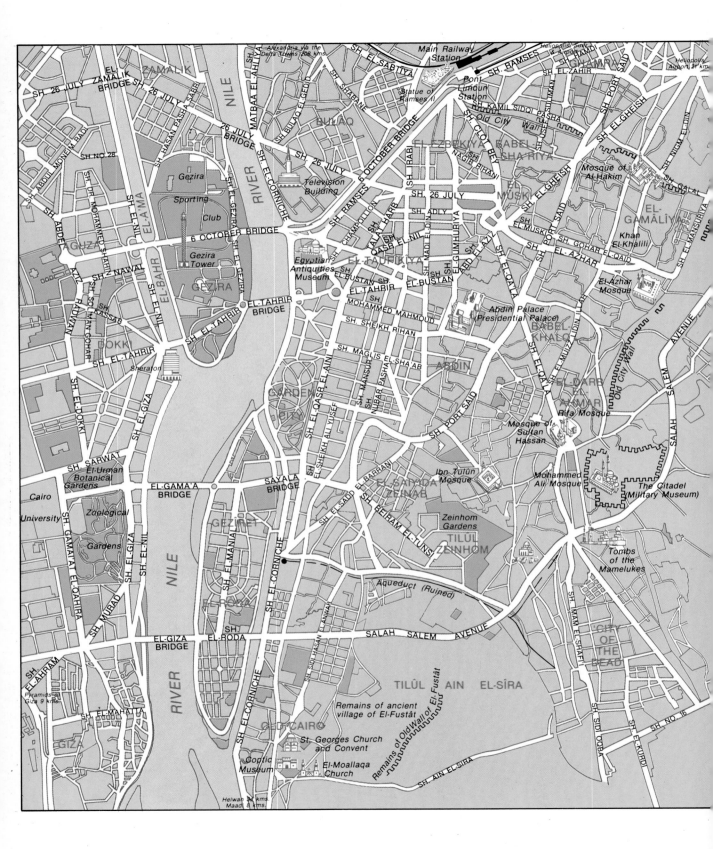